I Know Not What That Is

Destiny Johnson

I Know Not What That Is © 2023 Destiny
Johnson

All rights reserved.

Destiny Johnson asserts the moral right to
be identified as author of this work.

Presentation by *BookLeaf Publishing*

Web: www.bookleafpub.com

E-mail: info@bookleafpub.com

ISBN: 9789357742535

First edition 2023

Four

He is pulling mother down the stairs.
She is screaming loudly,
she is obviously in pain.

He goes back up the stairs.
He throws the dirty laundry basket
at her down the stairs.

She runs out the front door.
He picks up a screwdriver as the door slams.
He chases her out the door.

She throws the trashcan down in front of him.
She screams at him and dials 911.

He approaches, and she swings at his face.
He screams in agony.
His blood is dripping on the driveway.

Mother runs back in the house.
I sit in the floor and watch Finding Nemo.
Mother peeks in and sees I am okay.

Am I okay?
He should not touch mother.

I am sad.
She did nothing wrong.

We left him that night.
I have no toys.
I have no clothes.
My big house is gone.

I am not a normal girl; I know not what that is.

Five

He is your new daddy.
You are going to have a sister.

She will be pretty.
She will be smart.
She will be just like you.

He will be your new daddy.
He is not very nice.
He is mean to me and mother.

We have no money.
We have a tiny house.

I miss my big house.
I miss my toys.

He is mean to me and mother.
He spanked my little brother.
He is not very nice.
He told me I am stupid.
He told me I am worthless.
He is not a normal daddy.

I am not a normal girl; I know not what that is.

Six

I got off the bus today.
My new daddy was not here.
Mother says he did something bad.
Mother says he is in jail.
Mother says he deserves it.
Mother says he will not be mean anymore.
Sister was born.
Sister is smart.
Sister is pretty.
Sister is better than me.
We have less money.
We have a smaller house.
Mother says it will be okay.
Mother says we will be okay.
Mother says we are special.
Mother says we are smart.
Mother says sister will be just like me.
Mother is sad; mother is hurting.
Mother does not deserve sad.
I am sad with mother.
I am not a normal girl; I know not what that is.

Seven

"Your special milk will help you sleep very
soon."
"I am special?"
"Oh yes, you are a very special little girl."
I am paralyzed.
I am stuck.
The milk made me not move.

The door opens.
The light flashes in.
The door closes.
The light is gone.

He is here to help me.
He climbs on top of me.
He starts peeling my clothes off.
That is not how he should help me.
He should make the milk stop working.

I am special.
That's why I got the milk.
Why is he taking my pants off?
Why is he opening my legs?

It is cold in here.

My body is cold.
His hands touch my no-no square.
Why would he do that?

I am special.
"I'll pay double. Just like we discussed."

The door opens.
The light flashes in.
The door closes.
The light is gone.

Uncle is gone.
Pay for what?
Why is he touching me there?
He takes his pants off.

He bends down and kisses my forehead.
I see his no-no square out.
It is much bigger than my little brother's.
It is standing up too.

That is strange.
He climbs on top of me.
I cannot move.
I can feel what he is doing.
He is touching me.
He is going inside of me.

It hurts.
I cannot scream.
I cannot move.
It feels like he is stabbing me.
Is this what happens when you are special?

He stabs into me. It really hurts.
There is blood.
There is lots of blood.
I cannot move.

It is warm.
He puts his pants back on.
"Mother will go to jail if you tell. "

The door opens.
The light flashes in.
The door closes.
The light is gone.

I am bleeding.
I cannot move.
I never tell.
Mother should not go to jail.

I am not a normal girl; I know not what that is.

Eight

Sister always talks.
Brother always reads.
He is always in jail.

Aunt and cousins moved in.
Aunt got me in trouble.
Cousin did it, not me.

Mother says it is my fault.
Mother says I am the oldest.
Mother says she does not care.

Mother says not to wake sister.
Mother says get over it.
Mother says be a big girl.

Mother says it will be okay.
Mother says I am special.
He says I must not tell.

Mother will go to jail.
Mother does not deserve jail.
Mother did nothing wrong.

I am not a normal girl; I know not what that is.

Nine

It is only 9:30.
The door opens.
The light flashes in.
The door closes.
The light is gone.

I already know what is coming.
I am frozen.
I must pretend to sleep.
He smacks my face.
It stings like tiny bees.
I must not move.

He climbs on top of me.
He shoves my face into the pillow.
The air is thick and hot.
Just breathe.
He tears me open.

I bite my tongue.
I must not scream.
I must not move.
He tears me open.

I squeeze my eyes shut.

I must not scream.
I must not move.
He tears me open.

Hot sweat drips down my back.
I must not scream.
I must not move.
He tears me open.

I must pretend to sleep.
I feel the puddle of warmth.
He is finished.

It is only 9:45
The door opens.
The light flashes in.
The door closes.
The light is gone.

It is not over.
A single tear falls.
I am dirty.
I am not normal.
I must not move.

It is only 10:00.
The door opens.
The light flashes in.
The door closes.

The light is gone.

I already know what is coming.
I must not scream.
I must not move.
He tears me open.
I must pretend to sleep.

I am not a normal girl; I know not what that is.

Ten

School is hard.
I read the line.
I read the line again.
I can't read the sentence.
There are 49 questions left.
I am staring at an empty test.

I can't catch the sentence in my hand.
I can't hold the concept in my brain.
The clock runs out.
Time to submit.

Mom says I am special.
Mom says I can do better.
Mom says I am smarter than this.
Mom says I can be the perfect daughter.

I used to be smart; now I am dumb.
I used to be special; now I am broken.
I used to be perfect; now I am damaged.
I am not a normal girl; I know not what that is.

Eleven

It is only 9:30.
I already know what is coming.
It is dark.
The lights are off.

The TV is on in the background.
A little girl is still missing.
A little girl is dead.
The world is a bad place.
The world is a sad place.

It is only 9:45.
I already know what is coming.
Nothing has happened yet.

The door does not open.
The light does not flash in.
The TV stays on.
I must not move.
I am not normal.

It is only 10:30.
I already know what is coming.
Nothing has happened yet.
I must not move.
This is not normal.

It is already 12:30.
Nothing has happened yet.
I must be too dirty.
My eyes finally close.

It is already 7:30.
I jump up awake.
The door never opened.
The light never flashed in.
This is not normal.

The men never returned.
The door never opened.
The light never flashed in.
I live in a world of darkness.
I must be too dirty.
I am too dirty and broken.
Even he doesn't want me.

I am not a normal girl; I know not what that is.

Twelve

We have the same birthday, we have the same green eyes, we have the same friends. Why is she different from me? She has a crush on that boy, that is really weird. She is really pretty and sweet, boys are dirty and gross. Doesn't she know what they do? Doesn't she know they are bad? Maybe not all boys are bad. Maybe he is a nice boy, and I just don't know. Why don't I like boys? Because boys are bad. Boys hurt you. But maybe all boys aren't bad. I like girls more, though; she is really pretty. I like her more, but maybe she thinks I am gross. I am gross, why else would they have hurt me? I am not normal; I am not worthy of being liked. Maybe that boy is better than me, maybe I am more gross and more weird. I am damaged. Maybe she likes that boy because he is not damaged. He is not broken like me. We have the same birthday, we have the same green eyes, we have the same friends. The only difference is that I am damaged. He said nobody would ever want me. I know now he was right. She is a normal girl. I am not a normal girl; I know not what that is.

Thirteen

Grandpa passed away this weekend
I don't understand death.
Do you just leave?
What would it be like if I died?
Would anyone know?

Mother says death is bad.
She is very sad about grandpa.
I am jealous of grandpa.
I think she would be sad about me too.
Mother doesn't deserve sad.
Mother did nothing wrong.

I wonder what death is like.
Is death easier than life?
He can't find me in death.
Mother would not go to jail.
Mother would be sad.

I would be gone.
Maybe it is best that way.
No.

Mother would be sad.

I would be gone.
Would I still see stuff?
Would I just be asleep forever?
Is Heaven real? Is hell real?
Maybe someday I will find out.
But mother would be sad.

I am not a normal girl; I know not what that is.

Fourteen

"Do you like me?"
"I don't know."
"Do you think I'm pretty?"
"Yes"
"Do you want to be my girlfriend?"
"I am not allowed to date"
"He will never know."
"Are you sure?"
"He can't touch you anymore."
"Okay, I guess we can date."

"Why are you sad?"
"I am always sad. You are always sad, too."
"We can be sad together."
"I don't want to be sad anymore. Sad is not normal."
"What is normal?"
"I don't know. I guess sad might be normal."

I am not a normal girl; I know not what that is.

Fifteen

I told just one lie
"Nobody is hurting me"
Everyone lies once.

I am not a normal girl; I know not what that is.

Sixteen

I am good at pretending.
I am good at not saying.

I must not say a word.
I never say a word.

They believe I am just weird.
They believe I am just a stupid teenager.

I wish someone would just ask.
I wish someone would just wonder.

They tell me I am smart.
They tell me I can do anything.

Until I say I want to do things.
Then I will never be successful.

I wish they knew I am not normal.
I wish that they would see.

They know not that I am damaged.
They know not that I am broken.

There is no worse way of living,

than living a life in silence.

One day they may hear me.
One day my voice will be heard.

For now I must just suffer.
Suffer in the endless void.

Silence it is killing me.
Silence is just my normal.

I am not a normal girl; I know not what that is.

Seventeen

"I want to touch your body."
"He hurt me."
"I would never hurt you. I want to kiss you."
"I'm not allowed to date."
"You will be 18 soon. We can date then."
"I don't like boys. You are a boy.
But I like you. But you are a boy."
"If you like me, let me kiss you."
"He hurt me."
"I won't hurt you. I like you. Let me kiss you."
"Fine. You can kiss me."
"I want to touch your body. I won't hurt you."
"He hurt me. I don't like boys. Don't touch my body."
"Let me touch your body."
"He hurt me. I don't like boys. You are a boy. You touched me. You hurt me. Now you are gone."
"I only wanted to touch you. You are too damaged."

I am not a normal girl; I know not what that is.

Eighteen

He asked for a date.
The answer was yes.
Only a date.
He wants to touch me.
The answer is no.
Only a date.

He holds my face into the pillow.
He forces me.
He takes all my clothes off.
He ties my hands to the posts.

I am stuck; I must take it.
I must not move.
I must not scream.
He tears me open.

There is a knife; I bite my tongue.
I must not move.
I must not scream.
He tears me open.

He slaps my face; it burns like fire.
I must not move.
I must not scream.

He tears me open.

He bites my leg; warm blood trickles.
I must not move.
I must not scream.
He tears me open.

This is all I am good for; I am worth no more.
I must not move.
I must not scream.
I must take it.
I deserve it.
I am dirty.
I am damaged.
He tears me open.

His sweat drips down my back.
I must not move.
I must not scream.
I must take it.
I deserve it.
I am dirty.
I am damaged.
He tears me open.

I feel the puddle of warmth.
He is finished.
He unties my hands.
He pulls me from the bed by my hair.

He kicks my stomach.
He punches my face.
My nose bleeds.
He is in charge.

I must not move.
I must not scream.
I am damaged.
I am broken.

He drops me to the floor.
I must not move.
I must not scream.
I deserve this.

The door opens.
The light flashes in.
The door closes.
The light is gone.

It is not over.
I must not tell.
I never tell.
A single tear falls.

I am going to be a mother.
He is not happy.

He kicks my stomach.
He kicks my back.
He punches my face.
My nose bleeds.

I was going to be a mother.
He is not happy.
There is blood.
I am not going to be a mother.
She is gone.
She is a ghost.

I am not a mother.
I am not a person.
He hurt me.
He hurt her.
The window opens.

He grabs my hair.
He yanks me away from the opening.
He hits my face.
He kicks my back.
He throws me back to the floor.

The door opens.
The light flashes in.
The door closes.
The light is gone.
He is gone.

I want it to be over.
The window opens.
I am afraid.
Jumping is easy.
Why can't I jump?

A single tear falls.
I sink to the floor.
There is blood.
He hurt her.
It is my fault.
I let him hurt me.

I am not a normal girl; I know not what that is.

Nineteen

Another man comes,
another man goes.
Just another day,
just another night.

He comes in,
he uses my body,
he goes out,
he takes another piece of me with him.

This is what I'm good for.
This is what I'm worth.
Even the one that loves me walks away.
Even the one that loves me needs someone else.

He says it was a mistake.
He says I didn't deserve that.
I do not believe him.
I do not believe that I am worth anything.

They know that I can't tell them no.
They know that I don't know my worth.
They know that I am damaged.
They know that I am broken.

He begs me to learn my worth.
He begs me to believe him.
He tells me I am beautiful.
He tells me this is not me.

Maybe I finally believe him.
Maybe he's right about my worth.
Maybe I do not deserve this.
Maybe I can be a normal girl again.

No.
I am not a normal girl; I know not what that is.

Twenty

His arm is around my waist.
It is dark.
His beard is touching my ear.
There is lightning.
His breaths are light and sensitive.
He shifts and his arm pulls my hair.
His body is warm.
He feels nice.
His feet warm mine.
His hand holds my breast.
He cheated.
She laid here too.
He wanted her more.
He came back.
He chooses me.
She is gone now.
He is not a normal boy.
He will not hurt me.
He is tall.
He is smart.
He chooses me.
He does not choose her.
He climbs on top of me.
The answer is yes.
With him it is nice.

I might love him.
He does not love me.
He came back.
He chooses me.
He might love me.
He is not a normal boy.
He feels nice.
He is gentle.
He holds my hands with his.
It is big; it does not hurt.
It feels nice.
I am his.
He is mine.
There is lightning.
His sweat drips on my stomach.
A part of him is mine.
His touches are gentle,
his body fits perfectly with mine.
He kisses my ear.
He pushes into me with a gentle force.
He is holding my waist as leverage.
Kissing my lips,
he makes my body his.
It is warm.
He is finished.
He lays next to me again.
He rubs my head.
There is thunder. boom.
There is rain.

I love him.
He kisses my ear.
He loves me.
His arm wraps back around my waist.
I am damaged.
I am broken.
I am special.
I am fixed.
I am his.
I do not want it to be over.
I am not a normal girl; I know not what that is.

Twenty-One

The light gleams through the blinds.
I'm in bed alone tonight,
Happiness in that I find.

The man that loves me is just miles away.
But I am happy in my place.
Even these miles away, I know he will stay.

For once I see the colors,
For once I hear the birds,
For once there is more than what he said I'm
worth.

It's been a long time coming,
I've come miles from where I was.
The lights, the smells, the colors, they're all par
for the course.

I am not a normal girl; I know not what that is.

Twenty-Two

I walk out onto the back porch.
He follows behind me with a small paper bag.
In the bag I find a book.
"Our Adventure Book"
He is down on one knee.

I see a collection of photos.
A reminder of sad.
A reminder of hard.
A reminder of happy.
A reminder of easy.

A reminder that he loves me.
A reminder that I am enough.
I had a hard journey.
There will always be hard days.

I am a mother of a ghost.
I am a survivor of abuse.
I am the partner of a Prince.
My hands wrapped inside of his.

I am damaged.
I am broken.
I am special.

I am fixed.
I am his.

There is a diamond,
it is reflecting the blue-green sunset.
The smell of a spring breeze brushes by my
nose,
birds chirp around my in the trees.

"Will you marry me?"

I am not a normal girl; I know not what that is.
But if it were a normal girl, it would not end like
this.